TESTING  TIMES

WE'RE ALL IN TIGHTEN YOUR BELT THIS TOGETHER

Peter Brookes

\R^p\

The Robson Press

For Alba

First published in Great Britain in 2015 by
The Robson Press (an imprint of Biteback Publishing Ltd)
Westminster Tower
3 Albert Embankment
London SE1 7SP

Individual illustrations featured in this book were first published in *The Times*.

ISBN 978-1-84954-917-2

10 9 8 7 6 5 4 3 2 1

A CIP catalogue record for this book is available from the British Library.

Set in Baskerville MT Std

Printed and bound in Great Britain by
CPI Group (UK) Ltd, Croydon CR0 4YY

MIX
Paper from
responsible sources
FSC® C020471

INTRODUCTION
By Peter Brookes

They lay in a huge pile, blood everywhere, life oozing away: party leaders, Cabinet ministers, shadow Cabinet ministers and MPs. Elections show no mercy to politicians, nor, it would seem, to political cartoonists. The day after the result, *The Times* published a generous letter from a reader wanting to offer his sympathy at the loss of my 'two best gifts to the nation', and bemoaning that to lose both Wallace and Gromit, Miliband and Balls, in one electoral catastrophe was a tragedy for cartoon aficionados. Would politics, he asked, see their like again?

It was tragedy upon tragedy for me, as I also lost Cleggers, the fag to Cameron's head boy in my Westminster Academy public school cartoons. From being the victim of many a toilet shower in the school's loos, with gloating Tory prefects holding him down, Nick Clegg went one better on 8 May and actually flushed himself round the S-bend to political oblivion. What an extraordinary result. Three opposition leaders gone in one morning. Finito, kaput, banjaxed (though Nigel Farage later rescinded his resignation).

I've since tried to convince myself that the demise of Wallace and Gromit, and of Cleggers, was a good thing. After all, I'd been drawing these characters for five years (with a brief interlude for Alan Johnson as Gromit before he, too, threw in the towel), and wasn't I bored stiff with it all? Not a bit of it. Already I'm regretting the lost chance of skewering the plasticine pair in Nos 10 and 11, looking even more absurd as they attempt to operate the levers of power. It would have been pure cartoon joy to invent new methods with which posh Dave, the Flashman-like bully from *Tom Brown's Schooldays*, might torture and humiliate his coalition junior in a new term.

They were all wonderful to draw. I particularly enjoyed painting the details: the pattern of Wallace's green tank top, his tombstone teeth, and his panda eyes staring from their circles of black; Gromit with a paw over his eyes, unable to look at his idiotic master; Cleggers's ill-fitting school uniform, far too big for him, just like political office in real life; Cameron's union flag waistcoat and his sponge-bag trousers. Oh, I'll miss them all right.

Unfortunately, the campaign itself was in no way as momentous as the result and its consequences. No election can ever be dull, because it is politics at its most concentrated, and there is no other show in town. Readers are more engaged because of the heightened atmosphere. We even sell more papers. But this one managed to be duller than most. The campaign had, of course, been going on for months prior to the official launch on 31 March (the effect of a fixed-term parliament), so people were already suffering election fatigue before it even started. Politicians showed little appetite to confront their public, so anxious were they not to put a foot wrong. All gatherings were vetted and in front of known supporters. Consequently, very little actually happened. The TV debates were a substitute for political engagement; by their very nature they were highly stage-managed, so much so that interlocutor Jeremy Paxman emerged the winner of the first sterile bout between the two main party leaders. The only act of spontaneity in the whole shebang was Ed Miliband tripping over himself, symbolically, as he left the stage in the final debate. Coquettish Nicola Sturgeon emerged the star from it all, despite her appallingly negative message; hardly surprising when all else was such dross.

Where, in 2015, was the Gordon Brown/Gillian Duffy moment of 2010, when he was heard on air from his car, thinking his microphone was switched off, calling her 'a bigoted woman' (probably losing the election there and then)? Or the equivalent of the impressive Sharron Storer haranguing Tony Blair in 2001 outside the Queen Elizabeth Hospital in Birmingham over NHS failures? This time we were sleepwalking through an anaesthetised campaign because our elected representatives were scared of similar treatment. Yes, we had some moments: Defence Secretary Michael Fallon's attack on Miliband for being a backstabber; the latter's after-dark meeting with revolutionary Russell Brand in his luxury Shoreditch pad (where that daft kitchen tap seemed to grow out of Ed's head) in an attempt to hoover up the yoof vote (probably only an attempt, as most of RB's spotty adherents wouldn't have registered in time); and, of course, the infamous, truly ridiculous Ed-stone.

But these last instances were not the natural fallout from the rough-and-tumble of spontaneous political exchange. Because there was no exchange. No, they were self-inflicted wounds, and all the more pathetic for it. In such a bloodless campaign, it is surprising there was so much blood on the carpet.

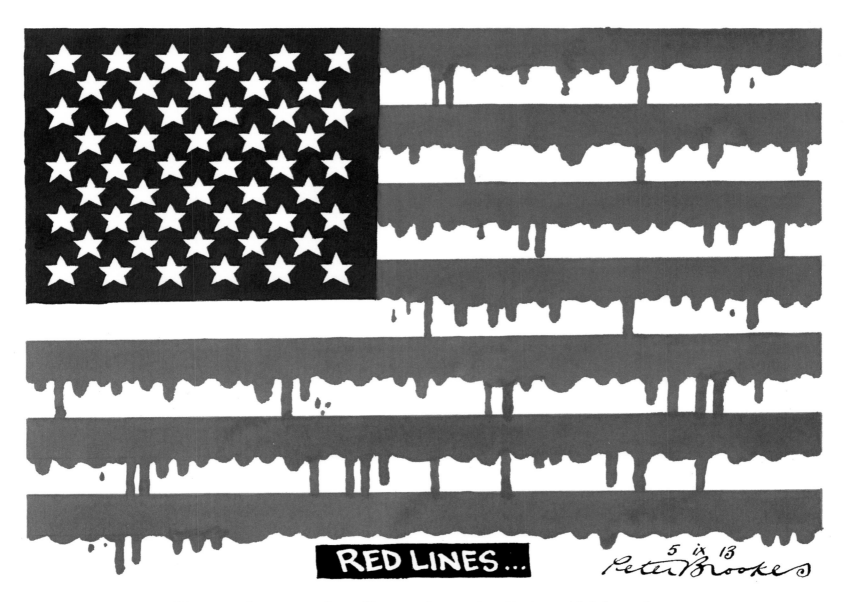

RED LINES ...

5 ix 13 Peter Brookes

Obama seeks support for military action against Syria amid debate about
the use of chemical weapons crossing a 'red line'.

Nick Clegg criticises single-party governments at the Liberal Democrat party conference, favouring further coalitions.

Ed Balls proposes alternatives to Conservative economic policies at the Labour Party conference.

3

David Cameron encourages Boris Johnson to return to the House of Commons in 2015.

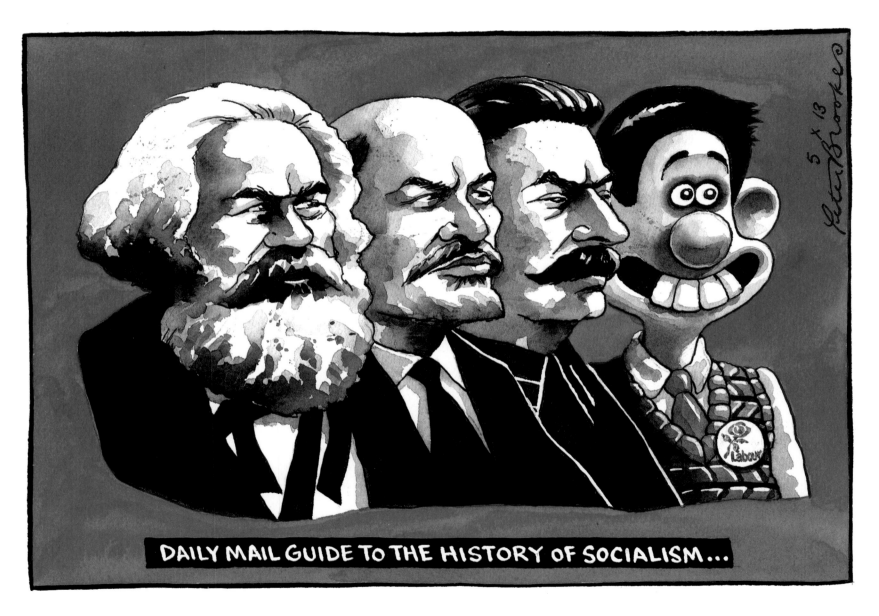

DAILY MAIL GUIDE TO THE HISTORY OF SOCIALISM...

The *Daily Mail* launches an attack on Ed Miliband's Marxist father.

George Osborne proposes a new system allowing Chinese banks easier access to Britain.

Angela Merkel questions Obama about the tapping of her mobile phone.

India launches a mission to Mars.

BAE Systems cuts 940 jobs in Portsmouth, sparing others in Scotland.

Cameron responds to John Major's criticism that the privately educated dominate positions of power.

Reports surface of looting by the survivors of Typhoon Haiyan.

RELEASE...

Nelson Mandela passes away, aged ninety-five.

David Cameron declares British forces will have achieved success by the time of their withdrawal from Afghanistan.

STARSHIP ENTERPRISE TO EARTH... ANY DECISION ON THAT THIRD RUNWAY YET?

The Airports Commission proposes methods to expand UK airport capacity, including a third runway at Heathrow.

The Gibson Report reveals British intelligence officers were told to ignore breaches
of the Geneva Convention regarding the treatment of detainees.

Nigella Lawson admits to drug use in a court case following her split from Charles Saatchi.

David Cameron claims Britain will face a wave of Romanian and Bulgarian immigration following the easing of labour restrictions.

Michael Gove accuses 'left-wing academics' and TV shows such as
Blackadder of distorting the history of the First World War.

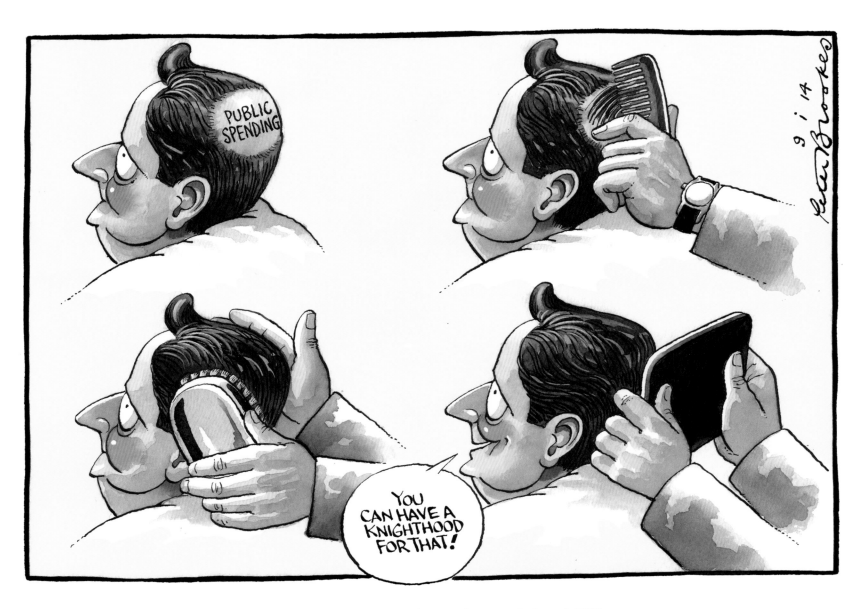

David Cameron's hairdresser is awarded an MBE.

Closer magazine reports details of an affair involving François Hollande and an actress.

François Hollande declines to answer questions about Julie Gayet in his first
press conference since his affair with the actress was revealed.

Cameron dismisses the US Defense Secretary's claims that proposed military cuts
would threaten the military partnership between the two countries.

Hiroo Onoda, the Japanese WWII soldier who spent nearly three decades hiding in the jungle before finally surrendering in 1974, dies, aged ninety-one.

Alex Salmond suggests Scotland could keep the Queen and the pound following a Yes vote for independence.

Michael Gove is criticised for engaging only with his own supporters
following his proposals for new education policies.

The Ipsos MORI Political Monitor reveals more Britons trust Cameron
than Miliband on the economy and unemployment.

David Cameron holds a crisis Cabinet meeting to discuss the inadequate
infrastructure preparation for recent flooding.

NICOLA STURGEON

MICHTY MOOSE SALMOND

DON'T LET GO

Mc GRAVITY

A BETTER TOGETHER CO-PRODUCTION WITH
ALISTAIR DARLING DAVE CAMERON GEORGE OSBORNE ED BALLS DANNY ALEXANDER MARK CARNEY (TECHNICAL DIRECTOR)
JOSÉ MANUEL BARROSO MARIANO RAJOY ANNABEL GOLDIE ED MILIBAND CHARLES KENNEDY BONZO DOG DOO-DAH BAND ETC

18 ii 14 — with apologies...

The second Scottish independence referendum debate is held. *Gravity* wins six awards at the BAFTAs.

The Times reports that the next Liberal Democrat manifesto will remove
policies to appeal to potential coalition partners.

Public sector employees are granted a below-inflation 1 per cent pay rise, though many NHS staff are excluded.

A UN report warns that the effects of global warming are likely to be 'severe, pervasive and irreversible'.

Nigel Farage and Nick Clegg participate in a televised debate over the
European Union, clashing over approaches to climate change.

The Queen holds a banquet in honour of Irish President Michael D. Higgins,
attended by former IRA commander Martin McGuinness.

Former Deputy Speaker Nigel Evans is cleared of sex abuse charges,
prompting calls for a review of the Crown Prosecution Service.

Jeremy Browne, a former Liberal Democrat minister, claims the party has
lacked relevance and clarity since forming a coalition.

Silvio Berlusconi is ordered to perform a year's community service with the elderly following his conviction for tax fraud.

ALIEN...

15 V 14
Peter Brookes
(in tribute to H R Giger,
creator of 'Alien', who has died.)

Nigel Farage suggests UKIP would be ready to support a Conservative
government on key votes in return for an EU referendum.

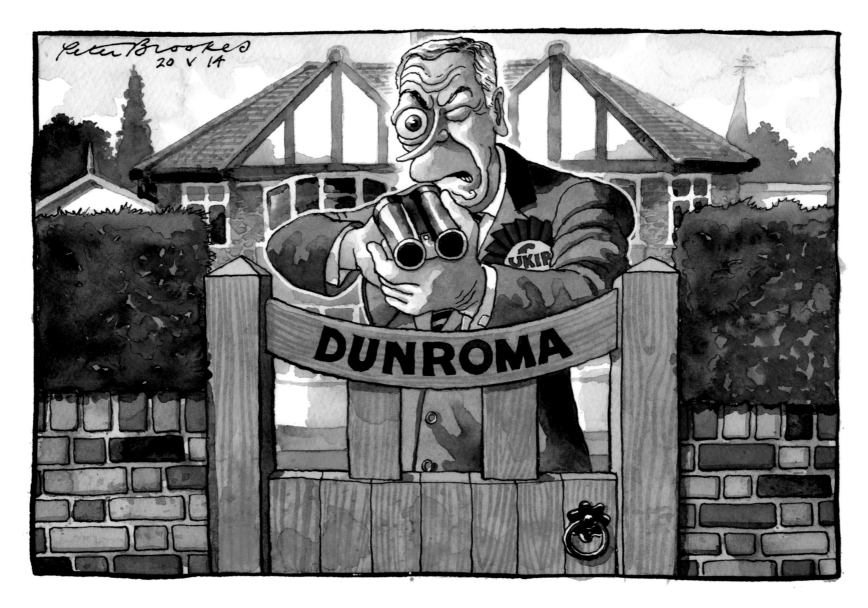

Nigel Farage sparks uproar with his comment that he would be concerned by Romanians moving in next door.

Cameron publicly opposes Jean-Claude Juncker's bid to be the next President of the European Commission.

Gove and Cameron announce plans to promote 'British values' in schools to combat Islamist extremism. The comedian Rik Mayall dies.

THE BLAIR PROPERTY PORTFOLIO...

GRADE II LISTED TOWNHOUSE...

MEWS EXTENSION...

COUNTRY PILE...

IRAQ: I WAS RIGHT

DUSTBIN OF HISTORY...

Tony Blair rejects claims that UK intervention in Iraq led to the crisis in the Middle East. The Blairs purchase their tenth property.

Ed Miliband proposes denying benefits to young people who refuse to complete training courses, as polling suggests voters doubt Miliband's ability to lead.

An Aberdeen man is identified in an Isis propaganda video, and Alex Salmond's proposed currency union faces defeat.

A review of the handling of historic child abuse cases is announced following the
revelation that a dossier from an inquiry into Westminster had disappeared.

A Malaysian Airlines jet is shot down near the Russian border with Ukraine, killing 298 passengers.

Three hospitals in Gaza are struck by Israel, which claims Hamas hide weapons in civilian structures.

THE MORAL HIGH GROUND...

A 72-hour Israel–Palestine ceasefire is agreed. Fifty-eight Israelis have reportedly been killed, including two civilians, compared to 1,390 Palestinians, thought to be mostly civilians.

Baroness Warsi resigns, stating she can no longer support government policy on Gaza, as Israel threatens a 'disproportionate' response to Palestinian rocket fire.

As David Cameron holidays in Portugal, Boris Johnson announces his decision to run for Parliament in 2015, encouraging rumours he could replace Cameron as party leader.

Cameron, Clegg and Miliband travel to Scotland to make a plea to the
Scottish people to vote No in the upcoming referendum.

Alex Salmond says Scotland is 'on the cusp of making history'.

Salmond sets out the case for independence in the final hours before the referendum.

At Labour's annual conference, Ed Balls claims the party has learned from
past mistakes and would be ready to make tough decisions.

MPs vote on whether to take action against Isis targets in Iraq.

Two more Tornado planes are added to the six already active in the strike against Iraq.

SPEAKING OF FREUD...

...AND WHEN, EXACTLY, DID THESE DELUSIONS OF BEING PRIME MINISTER BEGIN?

Ed Miliband launches an attack on the government over welfare minister Lord Freud's claims that disabled people 'aren't worth the minimum wage'.

The World Health Organization admits failures in its response to the Ebola epidemic.

Robert Iwaszkiewicz, an MEP of an extremist party associated with Holocaust denial, racism and misogyny, is welcomed into Nigel Farage's European Parliament group.

Miliband and Cameron bicker over their parties' respective immigration records ahead of a by-election in which the Conservatives are likely to lose to UKIP.

Polls suggest Labour will lose almost all of their Scottish seats in the
2015 election. *Mr Turner* is released in UK cinemas.

The government faces pressure over its failure to cut net migration, while Germany celebrates the twenty-fifth anniversary of the fall of the Berlin Wall.

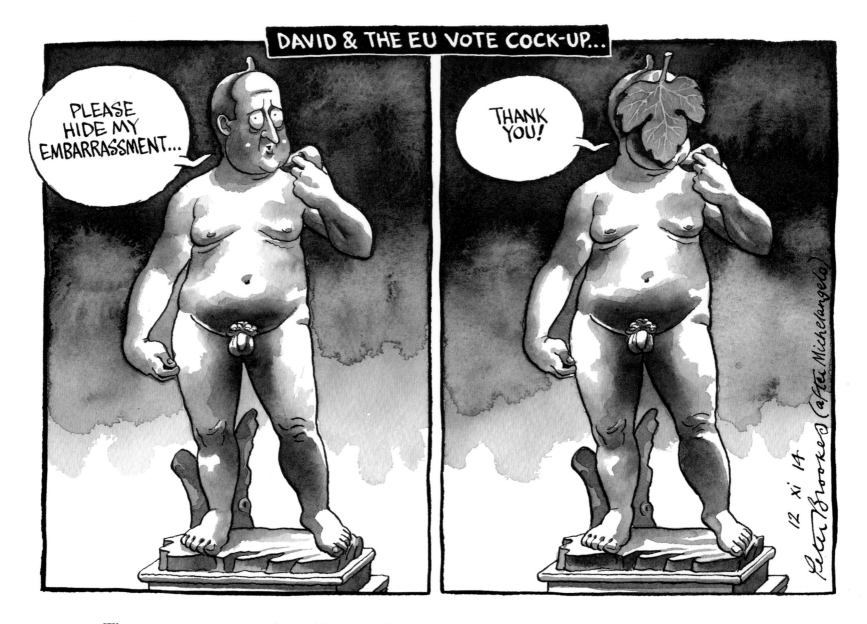

The government narrowly avoids a humiliating defeat in a vote on the European Arrest Warrant.

Nicola Sturgeon replaces Alex Salmond as leader of the SNP.

Theresa May appears on *Desert Island Discs* shortly before proposing new measures
to tackle terrorism which many claim threaten civil liberties.

A Senate intelligence committee report reveals the extent of the CIA's use of torture since 9/11.

A British man claims MI5 officers questioned him in-between torture sessions
inflicted by the Pakistani Inter-Services Intelligence agency.

Ed Miliband sets out Labour's plans for 'sensible reductions in public spending' in the next parliament.

The rouble falls to record lows.

TALIBAN VERMIN...

The Taliban attack a school in Peshawar, leaving 141 people dead, of whom 132 were children.

Relations thaw between Washington and Havana as Obama announces plans to normalise diplomatic and economic ties after more than fifty years of hostility.

Miliband begins his election campaign with promises to maintain the NHS without borrowing, as
a salvage operation begins on the stricken *Hoegh Osaka* cargo ship aground in the Solent.

CARTOON FIGHTBACK...

Eight employees at *Charlie Hebdo* offices are killed by gunmen who escape and are later killed during a siege.

Miliband accuses Cameron of cowardice after he refuses to take part
in a TV debate unless the Green Party are included.

Alexis Tsipras, leader of anti-austerity party Syriza, forms a coalition government
with Anel. Greek singer Demis Roussos dies, aged sixty-eight.

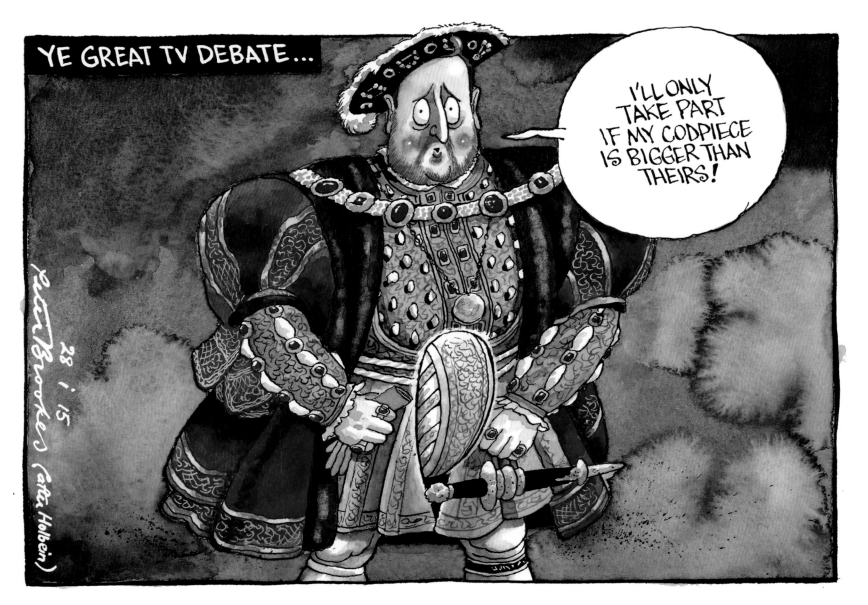

David Cameron faces pressure over his reluctance to commit to
pre-election TV debates. The BBC broadcasts *Wolf Hall*.

Leading universities attack Labour's plans to reduce tuition fees.

Ed Balls forgets the name of one of Labour's main business supporters on *Newsnight*.

The Liberal Democrats set out plans to make further welfare cuts if elected in 2015.

HSBC is accused of helping clients worldwide to avoid millions in tax.

The Conservatives hold an election fundraiser during which experiences with Cabinet members are auctioned off.

Nigel Farage proposes policies to ban unskilled immigrants from working in Britain following Cameron's failure to meet his targets on reducing net migration.

Nick Clegg reveals that the Lib Dem manifesto will include a pledge for drug law reform.

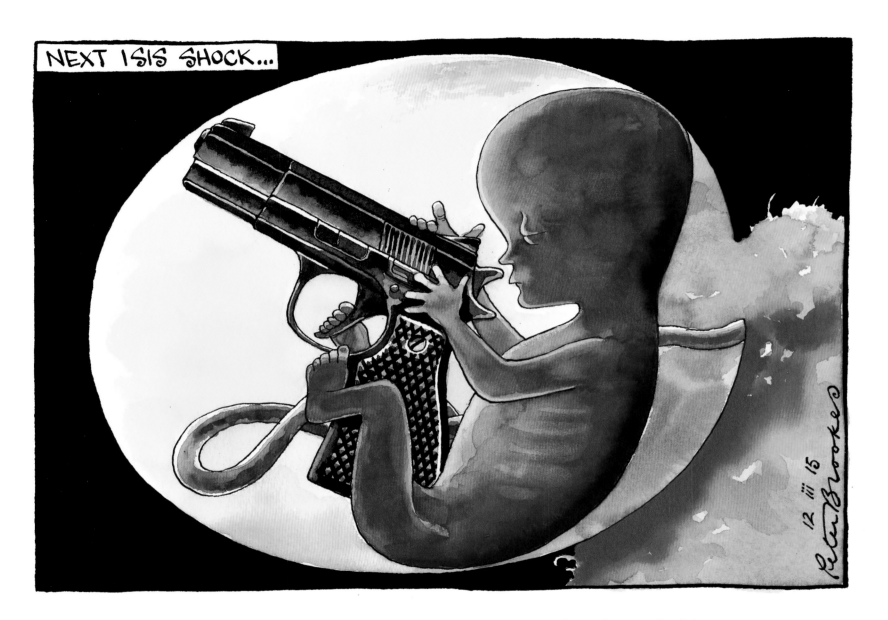

Videos emerge showing children as young as ten executing prisoners for Isis.

Miliband is photographed in a modest kitchen, later revealed to be one of two in his home.

Alex Salmond claims the SNP could hold the balance of power after the 2015 election. King Richard III is reburied at Leicester Cathedral.

Despite being dropped by the BBC after a physical attack on a colleague, Jeremy Clarkson remains hugely popular.

David Cameron launches the general election campaign on the steps of Downing
Street, urging voters to consider the Conservatives' success.

April Fool's Day.

Tony Blair claims that Cameron's proposal for an EU referendum would lead to economic chaos.

Michael Fallon claims Ed Miliband is 'willing to stab the UK in the back' by making a deal with the SNP on Trident.

Cameron is photographed feeding a lamb in his home constituency.

The Conservative Party launches its election manifesto, which extends the right-to-buy policy to 1.3 million families.

Leaders of the opposition parties participate in a televised debate, in which
Nicola Sturgeon challenges Labour to make an alliance with a bolder party.

Cameron claims that a nationalist party in government is a 'frightening prospect'.

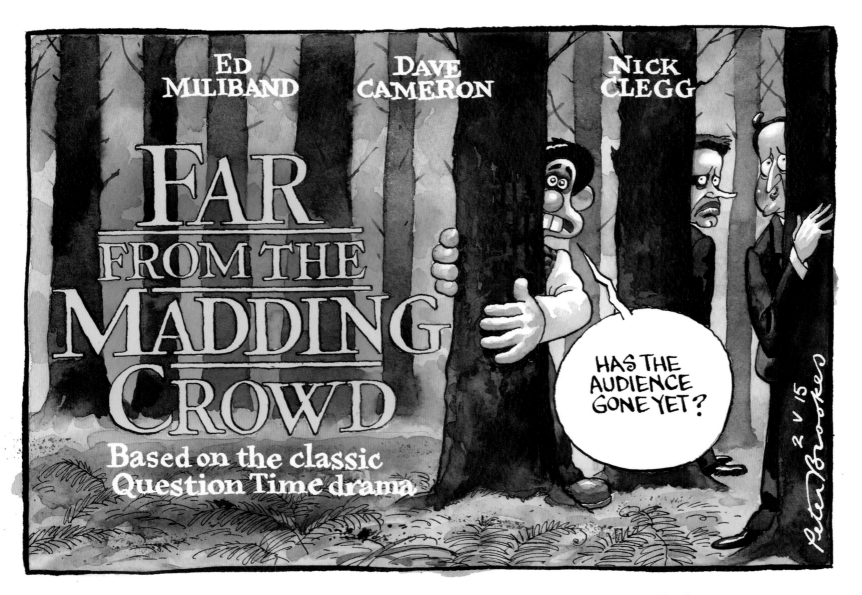

Cameron, Clegg and Miliband appear on *Question Time* in the final TV election
event. *Far From the Madding Crowd* is released in UK cinemas.

The election campaign enters its final hours, with all the polls pointing to a
hung parliament and a prolonged period of horse-trading.

A BETTER PLAN.
A BETTER FUTURE.

1 SEE IF THERE'S A
  JOB AT HARVARD.

2 OR THE LSE...

3 OR MAYBE
  TOP GEAR...

Ed Miliband

GRRR.I.P.

9 V 15

Peter Brookes

The general election results show a Conservative majority. Miliband, Clegg and
Farage resign as party leaders. Ed Balls loses his seat by 422 votes.

Farage's reinstatement as leader sparks in-fighting, with UKIP MEP Patrick O'Flynn calling him a 'snarling, thin-skinned, aggressive' man.

Andy Burnham is rumoured to have the backing of the unions in the run-up to the Labour leadership election.

Prince Charles meets Sinn Féin leader Gerry Adams. The prince's 'black spider memos' are published.

Sepp Blatter is re-elected as FIFA president.

Cameron rules out withdrawing from the European Convention on Human
Rights, against the advice of Justice Secretary Michael Gove.

Merkel suggests a deal can be reached over Cameron's demands for EU reform. Jilly Cooper's *Riders* cover is toned down for the thirtieth anniversary edition, sparking fierce debate.

Greece becomes the first developed country to default on a loan from the International Monetary Fund.

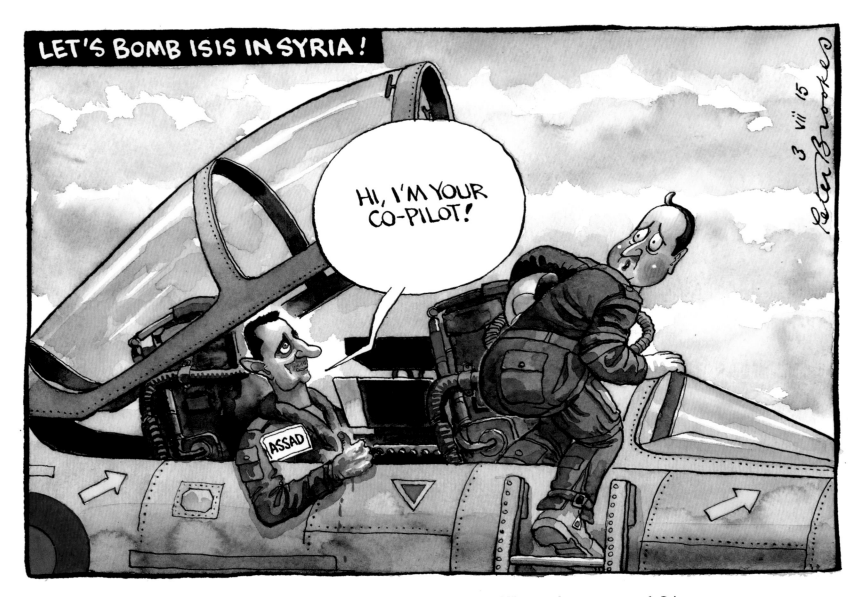

The Prime Minister and Defence Secretary call for UK warplanes to attack Isis targets in Syria, while critics warn against strengthening the Assad regime.

Greek voters decisively reject a proposed European Union austerity bail-out package.

IT'S A STEAL ...

George Osborne's first Budget of the new parliament adopts key Labour election
promises, such as abolishing non-dom status and raising the minimum wage.

PUBLIC ENEMY No 1...

23 vii 15
PeterBrookes

Aggressive seagulls attack residents in Brighton. Meanwhile, Jeremy Corbyn becomes
the unexpected front runner in the Labour leadership contest.